I WAS

MAD AT

GOD

I WAS MAD AT GOD

EMILE D. ETHERIDGE SR.

TATE PUBLISHING
AND ENTERPRISES, LLC

Published by Tate Publishing & Enterprises, LLC
127 E. Trade Center Terrace | Mustang, Oklahoma 73064 USA
1.888.361.9473 | www.tatepublishing.com

Tate Publishing is committed to excellence in the publishing industry. The company reflects the philosophy established by the founders, based on Psalm 68:11,
"The Lord gave the word and great was the company of those who published it."

Book design copyright © 2013 by Tate Publishing, LLC. All rights reserved.
Cover design by Joel Uber
Interior design by Jomel Pepito

Published in the United States of America

ISBN: 978-1-62510-430-4
1. Religion / Spirituality
2. Biography & Autobiography / Religious
13.11.18

Acknowledgments

The author would like to thank the following people for their tireless and dedication in helping in the release of this project:

Mrs. Melinda Etheridge
Mrs. Jean Wright
Mr. Ben Wright Jr.
Dr. Barbara A. Wright
Mrs. Frances J. Maust
Mrs. Vivian Hixson
Technical Adviser
Special Adviser
Adviser

APRIL, 1997

Sunday, the 27th, would be a day that would be one of darkest days in our lives. Melinda, my wife; the boys Justin (age eighteen), a freshman student at Penn State/ McKeesport College, and the baby boy Ian (sixteen), tenth grader at Laurel Highlands Senior High School; and I awoke to a day that we had never experienced before. Melinda and I talked enthusiastically about our oldest son, Emile Jr.'s, upcoming graduation from Juniata College on May 11. Melinda said, "What a great Mother's Day present that's going to be!" Then on June 28, Emile Jr. will celebrate his wedding day, the biggest day of his young life.

Personally, I was still enjoying the success of my first published book, an autobiography entitled *Can Emile?* As everyone readied themselves for church, I informed my lovely wife, Melinda, that I would not be attending service that day. The Lord placed on my heart to go to HealthSouth Rehabilitation Hospital near Pittsburgh,

Pennsylvania, once a month to visit my Christian friend Jeff Tarplay, who was in a terrible automobile crash that paralyzed him from the neck down. In the hospital, my heart ached for his physical state as he labored to breathe through his trachea. He requested ice chips from time to time from his daughter, mother, and father. I told Jeff to continue to progress so that we could share a pepperoni and cheese pizza. As I was getting ready to leave, a minister came by and had a prayer with us. I then left Jeff with his daughter, mother, and father at his bedside.

On my journey home, I decided to stop and visit with another friend, A1 Owens. After fifteen minutes of conversing, A1 informed me that Ben Wright's sister had a stroke.

I replied, "Al, Ben's sister is my wife! You have something wrong!"

"Oh, no," Al said. "It must be Ben's sister-in-law!"

Right then, I called my home, and I got no answer. I tried calling my brother-in-law and got no answer. I tried to call my mother-in-law and got no answer. I continued talking for about another fifteen to twenty minutes with Al. Then I started for home.

Upon my arrival, I found a note hanging from the door. The note stated, "Mom had a stroke in church. They had to Life Flight her to Presbyterian Hospital in Pittsburgh." Not knowing what to expect, my anxiety level shot up. I jumped into my car and was mad at God for allowing this to happen to my wife in his house. She was a pillar of the church, a trustee, a church clerk/secretary, the director of music, and the director of the Christmas cantata, not to mention a pillar in the community and a loving wife and mother. I screamed at God and said, "I am going to hold you to your promise that you would never leave us or forsake us!"

✦⟹⟸✦

Upon my arrival at Presbyterian Hospital, I could not find a parking spot, so I parked in a doctor's reserved spot. I ran into the hospital, and there was a long line of people. I made my way to the front of the line only to find that everyone was in line to sign in. I told the gentleman that I did not have time to sign in and that I had to get to my wife. He told me I was not going anywhere until I had signed in. As we became very loud, a police officer came over to see what the problem was. Then a lady at the head of the line told me that I could have her spot. I thanked the lady and rushed up to the eleventh floor, which was the intensive care unit (ICU).

When I arrived, I found all the family members in the waiting room. They were the ones who I was trying to reach earlier by telephone. They had a look of concern on each of their faces as they explained that Emile Jr. had arrived in two hours on what should have been a three-hour drive in order to sign a release for surgery for his mother. They said that I had just missed him because he was on his way back to Juniata College. Ben Jr., my brother-in-law, was the spokesperson for the family.

He told me that Dr. Yonas had operated and evacuated Melinda's skull. The doctor showed them the CAT scan and said that Melinda had massive bleeding in her skull, which was an intercranial hemorrhage with a lateral extension into the ventricles. Ben Jr. informed me that Dr. Yonas had said that the first seventy-two hours were crucial for Melinda to pull through. Dr. Yonas also said that he could not predict the outcome. Ben Jr. also explained the ICU visiting procedures, which were fifteen minutes every two hours and only two family members at a time.

By now, most of the family had started their journey back home to Uniontown. Justin had to take Ian home, and then he had to return to Penn State, McKeesport College. The ICU waiting room was about twelve feet by ten feet. I remember walking into the room and feeling the extreme anxiety from loved ones waiting for news. Two hours had passed, and a gentleman went over to a white telephone and dialed a number. When the telephone was answered, the gentleman asked if the Dzambo family and the Etheridge family could come back now, and they replied yes and buzzed the door so that we could enter. I walked into room 15A.

Upon seeing my wife, Melinda, lying there, clinging to life, I started crying uncontrollably, seeing her head partly shaved and incisions surrounded by stitches where Dr.

Yonas had operated. Her head was twice its normal size. She had two black eyes, tubes in her nose and mouth, her bottom lip was down to her chin, and there were IVs in her arms. I looked to my left and saw a machine breathing for my wife. I remember shaking my head and saying to God, "You said that you would never leave us or forsake us!"

I went back to the waiting room to find myself alone, crying uncontrollably once again. I struggled, trying to regain my composure. Once I got myself together, I got on the elevator. When I reached the bottom floor to the lobby area, I went directly over to the sign-in area and apologized to the gentleman for my behavior earlier. He accepted my apology and said he experienced it every day. I also apologized to the police officer, and he said he understood.

Just as I finished my conversation with the officer, I saw a familiar face that I could not put a name to. As I moved closer to exit the building, I asked her if she was from Uniontown, and she said "Yes, I work at the Laurel Bank where you do your banking." So we introduced ourselves. She said she was Tammy Adamovitch. I said I was Emile Etheridge. Tammy went on to tell me her husband was there due to some complications. I shared with her my wife's situation. Neither one of us knew what to expect, so we told each other we would pray for each other's spouses.

⊷⟾⊙⟾⊶

When I got to my car, I expected it to be towed away or have a ticket on the window. It so happened neither occurred. On the way home, I felt under so much pressure that I just kept asking God why. As I arrived home, I entered the house with a lonely and eerie feeling. I made my way up the stairs and went directly to Ian's room to check on him. He was in bed, asleep. So I went to our room and turned on the light to see an empty king-sized water bed. I lay on Melinda's side of the bed and decided that I would sleep there until her return. I lay there, looking at the ceiling, wondering what the boys were feeling, especially the baby boy, Ian, who was home with me. I thought to myself, *I must make it a point to talk with Ian when he awakens in the morning in order to give him an opportunity to express his feelings.* I was afraid to go to sleep not knowing if I could handle the enormous amount of pressure with decision making that would be awaiting me in the morning and in the days ahead. I thought for a second that if I were a drug addict, I would have overdosed, or if I was an alcoholic, I would have drank myself to death. If I were crazy, I would have gone to the highest bridge and just jumped off. I am blessed that I don't have any of these problems. I just needed God to lead and guide me, and I trust that he will.

⋆⇒◉⇐⋆

It seemed like I just shut my eyes, but it was time to get up. I went into Ian's room and found him awake.

I said, "What are your feelings about Mommy?"

"I have to keep working hard to make Mom proud," Ian said.

I told Ian I knew he would and then told him, "Ian, you know I will be gone a lot. I don't want anyone in the house, and I want you in the house by 7:30 p.m. Do you understand?"

He replied, "Yes, Dad."

I had to call Ms. Judy Means, our school board secretary, to inform her that I would be out of school a while and why. So I made the call, and she let me know that she would notify my building principal, Mr. Machesky. I told her I would keep in touch.

After getting off the telephone with Judy, it was about 7:00 a.m. I took my grade books to the home of Mr. John Seliga, one of my teaching friends, so the grade books could be given to my substitute teacher. Once again, I broke down while telling him that my wife had a hemorrhage that resulted in a stroke. He and his wife tried to console me by telling me that they would pray that everything would be all right. I left to pick up my mother-in-law, Jean Wright, who lives about fifteen minutes from our home. Then we started our two-hour journey down the Pennsylvania Turnpike. We prayed that Melinda would start showing some signs of improvement, but Melinda remained the same. It was like she was sleeping as the machines kept her alive. During the fifteen minutes we could be in the ICU, my mother-in-law and I were like two shepherds watching over Melinda as we continued to assure her that everything was going to be all right.

⊷⇛◉⇚⊷

Upon our return to the waiting room, we wept and prayed just like the others who were waiting. As we waited, we saw rescue helicopters coming and going, trying to save precious lives. There were about four families in the tension-filled waiting room, praying for the best. Mr. Dzambo had arrived and seemed to have a calming influence over all of us. He mentioned that Mrs. Dzambo was going to the step-down unit, which meant that she was doing well enough to leave the ICU. We all were so very happy. Also, that morning of the second day, the gentleman who cleaned the ICU rooms and the waiting rooms introduced himself to me and my mother-in-law. His name was Asa. He said, "I pray for everyone when I'm cleaning the ICU rooms. Your wife is in God's hands." I looked upon this man as a blessing because my faith foundation as a Christian had been temporarily shaken, and I was still questioning within my soul why this happened to my Melinda. I must say that Asa gave me a big faith-healing block to rebuild my temple of faith with his encouragement.

That afternoon, some of the staff from AJ McMullen Middle School came to the ICU waiting room just to show their love for my wife and me. It was truly a moving situation to see Mr. Machesky, the building principal; Mrs. Carol Kepps, the school counselor; and Mrs. Patsy Herring, the school secretary, who is a medical miracle in her own right. Some months ago, Patsy was stricken with a deadly illness that twelve other people died from. I recall when Patsy was in the hospital, some people said that it did not look good for her. As soon as I heard this, my faith would not let me accept it. I knew deep down in my soul that Patsy would recover by the grace of God. What a living testimony she is! During their visit, they brought reading materials. I was very appreciative.

That evening when I arrived home, I spotted a box of food delivered by my teaching friends. Upon entering the house, I found my son Ian in bed for the evening. So I sat down at the kitchen table, thinking about how a strong Christian upbringing would carry Ian through these troubled times. I made a conscious decision to put Ian in God's hands and to let him know that I loved him and that we would be there for each other. As I sat thinking, I looked down at the end of the table to see a stack of mail in which I knew there were bills. I looked at the stack then went downstairs and washed a load of clothes only to return upstairs to the same mail. The first piece of mail I opened was from Juniata College stating that if Emile Jr.'s last payment is not made before a certain date, he would not graduate. I continued opening the mail; it seemed like there was bill after bill. I took a break to put the food away that my colleagues had dropped off. Also in the box was money that was collected from around the school district to help my family with expenses. After putting the food away, I sat down to read the cards and then counted the money. I just started praising God. The money added up was to the penny of what Emile Jr. needed to graduate. The Lord had intervened; he took care of this bill. Keep in mind that Melinda had taken care of all the bills for all twenty-four years of our marriage. I had a big problem-solving project at hand. What do I do? I called on the Lord. I took out a tablet and listed every conceivable bill by name, the amount, and due date. I just shook my head and said, "How did Melinda do it?" I got the checkbook out of Melinda's purse. My lovely wife was the most organized person in the world. Keep in mind now, I have no clue how to write a check. Just then, I said, "Thank you, Lord" as I remembered my brother-in-law, Ben Jr., is the vice president of Laurel Bank. It was about 11:45 p.m., so I called Ben Jr., who is usually up at this time, and explained my situation. He said, "E, come to town. I would be more than happy to help you." I went downstairs and took the clothes out of the washer and placed them into the dryer before going to town. Ben gave me a 101 crash course in check writing, and I was very thankful. It took about one and a half hours. It was getting late, so I returned home about 1:15 a.m. and took the clothes out of the dryer, folded them, and put them away. By 2:00 a.m., I decided to bring this eighteen-hour day to a close. I had to get ready for day 4.

Wednesday, April 30, I awoke extremely exhausted, both physically and mentally. I went to town to pick up my mother-in-law and resumed our journey back down the Pennsylvania Turnpike to be with our loved one, Melinda. We prayed that this day would be better than the previous one. It seemed that there were new faces in that ICU waiting room. Every day it appeared to be a room of heartache. Our first visit with Melinda that day found her to be about the same. Aunt Carrie Turner, her son Nate, and his sister came and spent time visiting with the family. Thank God for our strong Christian family! Dr. Darryl Uphold, assistant superintendent of the Uniontown school district where I teach, came to show the love and concern for our family and also to represent Mr. Bums, the superintendent. Just as Dr. Uphold was getting ready to leave, Reverend Spence from Brownsville, Pennsylvania, came into the ICU waiting room and said, "I heard that there is someone in here from our area. Could we all have prayer together?" He was a blessing! Later that day, a Laurel Highlands School board member, Mr. Gary Carter, stopped by to see if we needed anything and if all was well. Our son, Ian, was a student at Laurel Highlands High School. Also that evening, Aunt Carrie's oldest daughter, Cathy, who lives in Pittsburgh, came by after work and spent the evening with us. Here is another family who loves the Lord. Cathy had prayer with us before she left. After Cathy left, we went in to see Melinda for the last time that evening to let her know God loves her and so do we. We went back up the turnpike to get a good night's sleep.

May, 1997

The next day was Thursday, May 1st, day 5. My mother-in-law and I started our journey down the Pennsylvania Turnpike, and I noticed the trees were beginning to bud. I brought it to her attention and said, "I pray that my babe would start to bloom." We arrived and went in to see Melinda for the first time that day. I noticed that the machine was just assisting Melinda with breathing. I felt that with our prayers, Melinda would start to bloom like the trees we had seen earlier. That afternoon, a doctor that specialized in tracheas came into the ICU waiting room and informed us that they would be inserting a tracheal tube into Melinda. They felt it would be better for her breathing and reduce the risk of infection. They had the surgery scheduled for the next day. We were enjoying our day with Melinda. She slept the entire day. More relatives from Smithfield came to see her. Aunt Donovan Tracey, cousin Joyce and her husband Walter, and Timmy and his wife Toni Tracey stayed for a while. Walter had prayer with us, and I thought to myself, *The power of prayer*! What a day! Then it was back up the Pennsylvania Turnpike for home.

Friday, May 2, Day 6, Jean and I started our all-too-familiar daily journey down the Pennsylvania Turnpike. The trees came to mind again as I said to myself, *Melinda is going to bloom.* By the time we had arrived, the doctor had performed the trachea surgery, and Melinda had been fitted with a size-8 tracheal tube. We were told that the surgery went well. As the day progressed, we noticed that the large family that had been in the ICU waiting room for several days was not there today. We discovered that the daughter had passed away. My heart was broken for that young lady; she was only twenty-six years old and had an eighteen-month-old baby. That evening, one of her family members came and was unaware of her passing. She sat there waiting for other family to arrive and seemed puzzled because no one was there. Finally, she went to the pay phone that was in the ICU waiting room and made a call only to find that her loved one had passed away. She appeared very upset, and I just put my head in my hands and cried and prayed that God would put his loving arms around her. Jean and I left brokenhearted for that family. It was a very long ride home. Jean asked me if it would be all right if she didn't come tomorrow, which would be the seventh day of Melinda's stay in ICU. Saturday was her clothes-washing day typically. "No, ma'am," I said. "I don't mind." I felt that this had been a strain on her. I told her that I thank God for her being there for her daughter and me.

The next day was, Saturday, May 3, which was the seventh day of Melinda's stay in the ICU. I started my solo journey, and the physical and mental exhaustion had set in. I pulled up to the tollbooth and sat for about three or four minutes, waiting for someone to take my toll ticket and money. I became agitated at the vehicles behind me for blowing their horns. Then it dawned on me that I needed to get my ticket to get on the turnpike. What a way to start the day! As I was driving, I had time to reflect over the week. I know for a fact that I kissed Melinda more and told her that I loved her more in the past seven days than I did during the last twenty-four years of our marriage. Right then, I asked the Lord for another chance by letting Melinda flourish like his trees were beginning to do up and down the turnpike. I remember my conversation with my mother-in-law. We both prayed that if the Lord would just let Melinda raise a finger, we would be ecstatic. I also remembered not seeing or meeting with Dr. Yonas that week, but I did inquire. One of his associates said that he was out of the country.

Before I knew it, I was at the hospital. I went in to see Melinda for the first time that day. I watched every movement on the left side of her body. I would stand there by Melinda's bedside for hours, wondering what she was thinking and what she was feeling. Not being able to communicate with her was agonizing and frustrating. I told myself that I should not lose sight of the fact that she had surgery and her brain was in the rebuilding stages. Melinda and I had a good day, so I started my journey home. Usually by the time I arrived home, Ian was in bed for the evening. I must say, Ian showed a great deal of maturity for a sixteen-year-old. I always tried to wash and dry a load of clothes at least twice a week. After doing the clothes, it was bedtime. It seemed that it was always after midnight or 1:00 a.m.

‹•⟺⟩ ⟨⟺•›

Well, the Lord woke me up to a day that I had never seen before, day 8 of Melinda's stay in the ICU, Sunday, May 4. I made it a point to sit down with Ian and have breakfast on the weekend just to listen to him. He said he was having difficulty in several classes. I told him to go to the school counselor and get a tutor for those subjects. I did not want him to feel any pressure from me, but I told him to do the best he could. He was participating in track, which I imagine was enjoyable and a release for him. He experienced success by breaking the school record in the discus. After our Sunday talk, Ian readied himself for church. I started my turnpike journey, and no, I did not sit there waiting to pay the toll. I was very much aware of what I was doing this time! That ride by myself just gave me time to reflect and pray that God would save Melinda.

As I reflect, she suffered from job-related hypertension. Recently, she reluctantly agreed to be the interim director of Fayette County's Head Start. Melinda was not very well received by her staff initially, but she was a firm and fair administrator. She would not even park in the director's parking space because she was the assistant director. She turned that program around and changed the staff's negative attitudes to positive, productive ones. Over the next few months, the staff pleaded with her to become the director, but Melinda said no. It was said that she insisted and demanded professionalism and accountability. After six months, a new director was hired, and Melinda returned to the assistant director's role, or so she thought. This new director came in and made it difficult for everyone. Melinda had expected changes, and she felt she could handle them and was a team player. I became quite concerned when Melinda would come home and say that everyone was becoming stressed out to the point of wanting to leave Head Start. The director sensed this and did not look at her as an ally but as an enemy. The new director started piling work on Melinda, having her redo work simply because she would reject it. I did not like what I was seeing and hearing from Melinda. I asked her to resign, but she said no way.

My concern became greater when I would come home from a basketball game to find her lying in bed, surrounded by paperwork from the office. I questioned her as to why she was putting herself through this. "I don't care how much she dumps on me. She will not get the best of me." Eleven coworkers concerned for her health told me that she never took lunch or any breaks and that she was losing too much weight. Something had to break. I was having thoughts of possibly losing Melinda.

The director called me at the ICU and suggested that since she lives in Pittsburgh that she could come visit Melinda. I was not rude in any way and told her that Melinda was not receiving any visitors. I have not seen or heard from her since that telephone conversation. I just put her in the hands of the Lord. She will have to answer to him one day. Before I knew it, I was at the hospital. The day with Melinda was enjoyable.

Every time I went in to see her, I would rub the left side of her body from shoulder to foot, looking for some sensation. It was time to start my journey home. Before leaving, I kissed my babe on her forehead and assured her that everything was going to be all right. As I drove home, I kept thanking God for not taking my babe away. I said to him, "I know that you are not done with Melinda!" I was soon back home for a good night's sleep.

I awoke the next day, the ninth day of Melinda's stay in the ICU. I went to town to pick up Jean, and we traveled down the turnpike to be with our loved one. Shortly after we started talking, we pulled into the hospital parking lot. We went in to see Melinda for the first time that morning to find she had been taken off the oxygen machine. She was breathing on her own! What a blessing! Dr. Yonas came in and introduced himself to me. He then went over to Melinda and said rather loudly, "If you can hear me, raise one finger up." Up shot one finger! "If you understand me, raise two fingers," said the doctor. She raised two fingers! Jean and I just started praising the Lord! Dr. Yonas took us outside of the ICU. "We have taken Melinda off the oxygen machine. She is just on compressed air and doing fine breathing on her own. But we have one concern: her cranial pressure. It is 46, which is in the critical range. We've performed three spinal taps. The first tap brought the pressure down to 32, the second tap brought the pressure down to 22, and the third brought it to 13. The spinal taps were spread out over several days." Then he said, "We may have to consider putting a shunt in to drain the fluid from the brain."

The Lord had answered our prayers. Let us remember that we had asked the Lord some days ago to let Melinda just raise one finger, and he allowed her to raise two fingers to let us know that she was aware. Yes, the Lord answers prayers in his time! He gave the sign of Melinda's blooming, and I knew there was more to come in his name. Dr. Yonas mentioned that they were going to have to place a feeding tube in Melinda's stomach to give her more nutrients and take away the risk of infection. What a day to be thankful for! It was now around lunchtime. Usually, Jean would pack a lunch for both of us, but she did not this day because she heard there was a cafeteria in the building. We left the ICU, and as soon as we turned the corner to go down the hall, we ran into a young lady whose name was Glenda Owens. She was a worker at the hospital. Glenda said, "I go in and pray for Melinda every morning when I come into work. There is something special about her."

We stood, praising the Lord and telling Glenda what a blessing she was to us. Glenda directed us to the cafeteria where we ate, and the food was very good.

On our return to the waiting room, we were so thankful and praising God. We entered the room to see another heartbroken person and sat next to her. My mother-in-law gave her some tissue while we proceeded to introduce ourselves. Her name was Londa Adams, and her husband's name was Mark.

I said to myself, *I hope and pray that Melinda continues to progress so she can get to the step-down unit, which would mean she would be out of danger. Being in this room day after day is heart wrenching.* What a day! We now knew that Melinda could communicate with her fingers. It was getting late, so we started our journey home with our hearts filled with joy, knowing the Lord had answered our prayers! As we drove, we reflected over this day, not losing sight of the fact that Melinda was recovering. Dr. Yonas was still concerned about Melinda's cranial pressure. It was still far too high, and that was why she was sleeping so much. If the brain does not start processing the fluid, they may have no choice but to install a shunt to drain the fluid. This would have to be monitored very closely in the days ahead.

They were also going to install a feeding tube in Melinda's stomach tomorrow.

During our conversation, it dawned on me that Emile's college graduation was coming up in six days. I thanked God for bringing it to my attention, and I brought it to my mother-in-law's attention. We were caught up in Melinda's day-to-day recovery. This very special day was now upon us. I went on to tell my mother-in-law that this was the last conversation that Melinda and I had on April 27, the day she fell sick. I told her how my Melinda had said that this was going to be extra special in that May 11 was Mother's Day as well as Emile Jr.'s graduation day. My mother-in-law decided right then that she would be with Melinda. I felt so hurt that Emile Jr.'s mother was not going to be there. I know without a doubt my wife would want Ian, Justin, and myself to be right there, and we were going to be there. Before we knew it, we were at my mother-in-law's doorstep.

Day 10, after a good night's sleep, my mother-in-law and I began our journey back down the turnpike, anticipating another great day. As we were riding, I made mention that when Melinda went to the step-down unit, I was going to go back to school. Up until this time, I had been out for seven days. My plan was to take one day at a time. We arrived at the waiting room and sat down next to Mrs. Adams, who was still visibly upset. She told us that they were still watching her husband, Mark, very closely. Like

Melinda, his cranial pressure was also very high. Our first time to see Melinda, she was asleep. We started talking, and she tried to open one of her eyes. We asked her if she knew who we were. We told her to raise one finger for yes and two for no. I asked her if she knew I was her husband, and Melinda raised one finger. Her mother asked her if she knew she was her mother, and Melinda raised one finger. We were so pleased. We would rub the left side of her body, looking for movement. We made sure not to burden Melinda with questions. We spent a good day with Melinda, and before we knew it, it was time to leave. So we went in to see Melinda for the last time this day. We reassured her that God loved her, and so did we. We left like always—with a kiss. We went back up the turnpike and headed for home.

Several days had gone by, and Melinda was in stable condition, but her cranial pressure was still a concern. Dr. Yonas informed us that over the past few days, they had to give Melinda two more spinal taps. She has had a total of five.

They were trying to get the fluid to an acceptable level. They started sitting Melinda up in hopes that the brain would start absorbing and processing the fluid. By this point, this was day 14 for Melinda in the ICU. On May 10, we learned that Mark Adams had been moved to the step-down unit. My mother-in-law and I were so very happy, and we just thanked the Lord. We were one day away from Mother's Day and our son's special graduation day from college. My brother-in-law, Ben Jr., was going to take the boys and me to Juniata College to witness Emile Jr.'s graduation. Well, once again, it was time to go in for our last visit with Melinda and to give her and her mother their Mother's Day cards. I read my babe her card and explained that I would not be coming with her mother tomorrow, which was Mother's Day. I explained that Justin, Ian, and I would be going to Emile Jr.'s graduation. We also let her know that Ben Jr. would be taking us. I asked Melinda if she understood, and she gave us a thumbs-up. My mother-in-law and I just looked at each other and said, "Thank you, Lord."

What a day. My mother-in-law said to me that Preston, her youngest son, would be bringing her to the hospital in the morning. Once again, before we knew it, we were home. I wished my mother-in-law a happy Mother's Day and said good night. Then I went home to get ready for Emile Jr.'s graduation. Our middle son, Justin, had come home from his college that evening. We were all set for tomorrow. We all awoke to Mother's Day, May 11, Melinda's fifteenth day in the ICU of Presbyterian Hospital and Emile's graduation day—two big days in one. We heard Ben Jr.'s car horn. Well, off we went up the turnpike, the opposite way from Melinda. We had a three-hour ride ahead of us. I thought it was very nice of my brother-in-law, Ben Jr., to take Justin, Ian, and me in his beautiful big new car. We were laughing and having a great time. We stopped and ate breakfast, and we started back on our way.

My emotions were so torn between happy and sad, but I had to stay strong for Justin and Ian. We were about one and a half hours into the drive when the car started sputtering and came to a stop. The first thing that came to mind was that we were out of gas, but the gauge was on full. The second thing that came to mind was that the car overheated, but the gauge was not registering hot. Then the thought of not getting to my son's graduation just made my heart start pounding. We sat there for a while. Ben Jr. had a cell phone, so he called AAA. They came and towed the car and us to the nearest garage. It did not look good for the car to continue on, so Ben Jr. called his lady friend, Dr. Barbara Chandler. She drove her car to us, but there wasn't enough room for all of us. So I drove Barbara's car, and she stayed with Ben Jr. at the garage with the car. When Justin, Ian, and I arrived at the graduation ceremonies, it was too late. Everyone was dispersing. We found Emile Jr., and I explained our car problems in getting there. Emile Jr. said he was looking for us. As he was talking, tears were welling in his eyes. He said he thought something was wrong. We hugged him, congratulated him, and told him how proud we were of him. I told Emile Jr. that I explained to Mommy where we were going today and that she gave me a thumbs-up sign. I said, "Let's go eat."

We went to our favorite place, which is Hoss's Family Steak and Sea House. As we were eating, we brought Emile Jr. up to date on Mommy's health situation. Emile Jr. went on to inform us that he had a summer job at a camp for disabled youngsters and that the wedding was still on for June. Everything with Jennifer was well in Texas. She was wrapping the school year up and getting the final details for Emile Jr.'s teaching job in Texas in the fall. Also, she was making preparations to come home for their wedding day, which was about a month and a half away. After eating, we went back to Juniata to Emile's dorm. I gave him a hug and told him that God loves him, Mommy loves him, and so did we. Ian, Justin, and I started our journey back home. We stopped at the little town where Ben Jr. and Barb were staying. Ben Jr. had checked into a hotel. He and Barb were going to stay with the car until the next day.

The boys and I started on our journey again. We were talking about how we were very family oriented and how it just did not seem right without Mommy. She was the catalyst. She organized everything. So we agreed that we would just keep praying that Mommy would get better and be able to go to Emile Jr.'s wedding. Well, there we were back home. As soon as I got in the house, I called my mother-in-law to see how the day went. She said that they had Melinda sitting up several times. I was pleased to hear the good report. So I told her that I would tell her how everything went the next day. When I picked her up, it seemed like the night had gone by so quickly. I began telling my mother-in-law about what had happened. She felt so bad that we had missed the graduation. I said, "Let's just pray that our babe gets well enough to be there for Emile Jr.'s wedding."

Well, there we were at the hospital on Monday, May 12. It was Melinda's sixteenth day in the ICU. During our first visit of the day with Melinda, Dr. Yonas came in and stated, "Tomorrow we are going to let Melinda go to the step-down unit, and we are going to keep a very close eye on her cranial pressure, and she will continue with compressed air." He showed us another CAT scan of Melinda's skull and where the bleeding occurred. Dr. Yonas went on to say, "As for the trachea and feeding tube, all is well." We were so very happy that we could not do anything but praise God. We went back to the waiting room on cloud nine. Asa, the cleaning gentleman, came into the ICU room, and we shared that good news with him. All he said was "Praise God." On our way to lunch, we saw Glenda Owens, the technician who goes in every morning to pray for Melinda. We shared our good news. She also said "Praise God." Glenda said that she would be keeping track of Melinda's progress.

After a good lunch, I told my mother-in-law that I was going down to the eighth floor to the step-down unit to visit with Mark and Londa Adams. She said okay and went back to the waiting room. When I knocked on the door, Mrs. Adams responded, "Come in." When I walked into the room, she introduced me to Mark. Londa went on to say, "I've been telling Mark about you and Mrs. Wright." I told Mark and Londa the good news about Melinda coming to the step-down unit. They were happy for Melinda, and both said, "Thank God." Mark told me that he might be going home later on that week. I told Mark and Londa we would see more of them when Melinda came down. I went back up to the waiting room.

I was sitting there for no more than five minutes when an older woman sat down beside me and introduced herself to me as Eleanor, the social worker. She asked me if I could come down to her office. Eleanor informed me that I should begin looking for a skilled nursing home for Melinda. I was taken aback; in fact, I looked at this statement as a step backward. I listened as Eleanor told me about the skilled nursing homes around Uniontown. She mentioned Laurel, Cherry Tree, Mount Saint Macrina, and Fayette Health Care Center. She said that she would make phone calls to see if there were any vacancies. I told her to feel free to call, but that's not what I had in mind for Melinda. I was thinking rehab hospital. Eleanor was insistent. Melinda should be placed in a skilled nursing home. She was persistent, stern, and very abrasive. It just did not sit well with me. So after her telephone calls, she informed me of the facilities that had openings. She did not seem very pleased that I did not submit to her plan. I told Eleanor that I would have to do some research and get back to her. She reminded me that a decision would have to be made soon.

I went back to the ICU waiting room and talked with my mother-in-law. At one point, I asked, "Lord, is this what you want for Melinda?" We felt that the Lord wanted more for our loved one. If he did not, he would have had me say yes to Eleanor. We felt that a nursing home for Melinda would be a dead end. My mother-in-law mentioned a rehabilitation hospital in Morgantown, West Virginia, that our aunt Naomi had gone to after her aneurysm. The family spoke so very highly of it. Just as we were talking, the Lord reminded me of the card that I had in my wallet from where my Christian brother Jeff Tarplay was staying. I pulled out my wallet, and there was the card from HealthSouth Rehabilitation Hospital of Monroeville. I went to the pay phone in the ICU waiting room and called the number on the card. I asked to speak to someone regarding placement. I explained our situation to Alice, the lady that I spoke with, and she said that their facility would not suit Melinda's needs. She also said I needed to find for my wife a facility that had a subacute unit. I had never in my life heard the term *subacute*. Alice explained that Melinda was not able to withstand three hours of intense therapy, so she would need to go into a subacute type of unit. She gave me a 1-800 number for the rehabilitation hospital in Harmarville, Pennsylvania, and to another rehabilitation hospital in Morgantown, West Virginia. I thought to myself that this was the hospital that Aunt Naomi went to and was so very pleased. Alice gave me a name and number of Ann Ciotoli, a liaison for HealthSouth Rehabilitation Hospital. She goes to Presbyterian Hospital, where Melinda was. I thanked Alice for her wealth of information. I got off the telephone and shared all the information with my mother-in- law.

I said the decisions we make could affect Melinda for the rest of her life, so we had to call on the Lord for guidance and direction. I said to myself, *Lord, I'm holding you to your word. You said you would not leave us nor forsake us.* We were still excited about Melinda going to the step-down unit. My plan was to return to school since my babe was out of serious danger. So I called the school district office from the ICU waiting room to tell them that I would be returning tomorrow. I was out of school a total of twelve working days. I felt that I needed some type of diversion from the pressure. I questioned myself if I was doing the right thing by going back to school. At the end of the school year, things needed to be put away, and grades needed to be done. But on the other hand, there was still a lot of work to be done in behalf of Melinda. My mother-in-law said that my father-in-law would take her to the hospital tomorrow. We went to see Melinda to look at her; she didn't look like my babe with all those temporary deformities. We are so thankful that we still have her. After our fifteen-minute visit, I felt compelled to call Ann Ciotoli to inquire about Melinda's possible placement.

I called and left a message on Ann's voice mail. I told her that we were looking to have Melinda placed at Mountain View or Harmarville. "Melinda at the present time is at Presbyterian Hospital in the ICU. She will be going to the step-down unit on the eighth floor tomorrow, May 13. Please contact me, I am Melinda's husband. My name is Emile Etheridge." I then called the 1-800 number for HealthSouth Mountain View in Morgantown, West Virginia. I spoke with Rhoda Dulany, who was the rehabilitation liaison. I explained my situation regarding Melinda. I told her that we really would like to get Melinda in there. Rhoda asked questions about Melinda's SelectBlue insurance and her condition. Rhoda told me she would check and get back to me in ten minutes. She did just that. Rhoda said that Melinda's SelectBlue was out of their network. I asked Rhoda if they had a subacute unit. Her answer was no. I went on to tell her that we had an aunt that was at Mountain View and that she spoke very highly of the facility and Dr. Biando. Rhoda asked what her name was, and I told her it was Naomi Wright. She said she recognized the name. I thanked Rhoda, and she said that if she could help in any way to please call her.

After that conversation, I was really down. The Lord told me to call the other 1-800 number, which was HealthSouth Harmarville in Pennsylvania. I called, and when the receptionist asked how she could help, I explained Melinda's situation and that she had an intercranial hemorrhage with a lateral extension into the ventricles. She referred me to the head injury program. The lady answering the telephone introduced herself as Donna Sebastian Van Kirk, program director of the head injury program.

The first thing out of my mouth was "Do you have a subacute unit?"

She replied, "We call it the transitional rehabilitation unit."

I replied, "Great!"

I explained that I was looking for a rehabilitation hospital that would meet my wife's needs. I asked Donna to give me directions to their facility and thanked her. What an emotional roller-coaster ride that was. One minute you're up, the next minute you're down. I just thank God for seeing me through it. I got off the telephone and shared the information with my mother-in-law. I am very blessed to have Jean Wright as my mother-in-law. I have been married to her daughter for twenty-five years, and I have never had a cross word with her to this day. She has been my closest confidant. We thank God for being God, for seeing us through the troubled times. We went in to see our loved one, Melinda, a few more times before calling it a night. I went down to the parking garage to get the car; before I knew it, we were home. Ian was awake, so I informed him about what was going on to keep him abreast. I was so exhausted mentally and physically. I knew I had to change gears before going back to school tomorrow.

May 13 was Melinda's first day in the step-down unit. I just needed the Lord to keep restoring my strength. When I awoke, Ian and I had breakfast together. It was great to spend a few minutes with Ian before he had to go to school. I told him to have a great day. Shortly after Ian left, I went to my school. I felt very good about being back. I went into the office to sign in. Our secretary, Patsy Herring, greeted me with a good-morning and said, "Nice to have you back, Mr. Etheridge." She asked me how my wife was doing. The emotional floodgates opened as I struggled to get "Fine" out. I left the office and went to the gym to get myself together before going to my morning duty in the cafeteria. On my way down to the cafeteria, teacher after teacher would ask me how my wife was. I would nod my head yes for "Okay" and keep walking. They could see I was out of it emotionally. As I entered the cafeteria, I struggled to keep my emotions in check. I admitted to myself it was just too much. I had made it through the day. I went home and called Mr. Macheskey, the principal, to tell him that it was just too much. He said he understood and for me not to worry and that everything would be all right. I just knew that I could not finish out the school year. I tried to lie down, but my mind would not let me rest. So I called the hospital to find out how the day went for Melinda. She was on the eight floor, room D-854. My mother-in-law said that the day went well.

I started dinner for Ian and me. When Ian came home, we talked about school and track. I told Ian that I would not be going back to school because I had to work for Mom full-time. He said that he understood. I started thinking about Eleanor, the social worker at the hospital, and that she said I should put Melinda in a skilled nursing home. I decided tomorrow I would be visiting skilled nursing homes. So I went to my closet and pulled out my best Sunday suit and pressed it, and I pulled out a white shirt. I shined my wing-tip shoes, and I sat down with a notepad and started formulating questions on skilled nursing homes that I needed answers to.

May 14 was Melinda's second day in the step-down unit. The first skilled nursing facility I went to was Laurel Nursing and Rehabilitation Center. I went to the director's office on a fact-finding mission. I spoke with Ms. Adieu. I told her that I was looking for a possible site for a loved one. I asked the following questions:

1. Did they have a resident doctor on staff?
2. Did they have inwall oxygen / compressed air?
3. Did they have a resident respiratory therapist?
4. What were their procedures for suctioning and bagging trachea clients?
5. What was their nurse-to-client ratio?

6. What was their procedure for caring for clients with feeding tubes?
7. How many times do they turn the clients per shift to prevent bedsores?
8. How many times do they change clients that are incontinent per shift?
9. How many clients do they have per room?
10. Do they have any clients who are age appropriate to room with my wife?
11. How are medications administered to trachea clients?

Then I requested to meet with the persons in charge of physical therapy, occupational therapy, and speech therapy. I had additional questions for each department head.

The second place I went to was Cherry Tree Nursing Center. I spoke with Ms. Christie Grimm. The third place I visited was Mount Macrina Manor. I spoke with Gretchen Geruschat. The fourth place was Fayette Health Care Center. I spoke with Ms. Jaimey Kuritz. Two of the four facilities asked me if I was from the state department. I said, "No, I'm just looking for a possible site for my wife." They said that they were very impressed with my professionalism and the type of questions I asked. After visiting the facilities in Uniontown, I drove down to HealthSouth Harmarville Rehabilitation Hospital near Pittsburgh. This is a rehabilitation hospital that had the transitional unit. Upon my arrival, I went to the head injury department and asked to speak with Donna Sebastian Van Kirk. She was in her office and agreed to speak with me. Donna remembered me from our previous phone conversation. She asked me to refresh her memory about Melinda's insurance. During our conversation, Donna felt that Melinda would qualify for their transitional unit. She was nice enough to provide me with a tour of their facility, and I was very impressed with what I saw. I proceeded to thank Donna. It was a very productive and informative day. I readied myself for the journey home. During the journey, I had time to reflect over the day, and I was very pleased.

Later that evening, I spoke with my mother-in-law to see how the day went. She informed me that they had given Melinda another spinal tap, which made this her sixth one. They were checking her cranial pressure. They found it to be at an acceptable level. I responded, "Praise God." That meant that Melinda would not require a shunt to drain the fluid from her brain. She also said that the day went well and that Melinda would be going to a regular room on the seventh floor tomorrow, and this was great news. I went to bed for a good night's sleep.

⋯⇒◯⇐⋯

I awoke the next day, Melinda's nineteenth day at Presbyterian Hospital. I drove over to get my mother-in-law for our drive to Pittsburgh. We talked about Melinda going to a regular room on the seventh floor. We were so very happy that Melinda was out of the step-down unit and would be placed in a regular unit. Upon our arrival, we stopped at the information desk to find out what room Melinda was in. She was in room 735 B. We walked into her room and found her resting. We were not there long before someone came to take Melinda to therapy. My mother-in-law and I went along. The therapist worked with Melinda's range of motion with her legs. We could see that Melinda's left leg was visibly limp. We were praying that the mind and body would come together. They put the splint back on Melinda's left foot to keep the foot from dropping. Then they took Melinda over to occupational therapy. They worked on her upper body, impartially with her left hand and her upper arm with range of motion. They paid very close attention to her blood pressure. They worked on trying to get Melinda's back muscles strengthened and to keep her head erect to stop her from drooling. I was concerned about Melinda's eyes. They were pulling to the extreme right. I asked the therapist about this, and she said that Melinda may have left neglect and said that her eyes would come back over in time. We could see that Melinda was very tired at the end of therapy. The therapist said that they were going to make a left-handed splint for Melinda. When Melinda had finished her therapy, we headed back to her room.

The social worker was waiting to talk about placement for Melinda. I suggested that we go to her office, and she said okay. When we got there, I told Eleanor that I had visited all of the skilled nursing facilities that she had told me about. Eleanor was startled. "You visited all of them?" I replied yes with a smile. My choice was Harmarville Rehabilitation Hospital. I told her that I had done my research. Eleanor said that time was running out and a decision must be made. I told her that I needed more time, and she was visibly upset. I went back to Melinda's room to share the conversation with my mother-in-law. I had just started talking when there was a knock at the door. I answered the door to find Ann Ciotoli, the rehabilitation liaison for HealthSouth Rehabilitation Hospital in Harmarville. She said, "I got your message on my voice mail. I've been trying to track you down." She said that all the information that I had given her sounded like Melinda would be eligible for placement. She also informed me that she checked with Harmarville's transitional unit, which is the same as a subacute unit. She said that they had openings. I told Ann that I would inform Eleanor the social worker that I wanted Melinda placed at Harmarville. I said to Ann, "I thank God for you." I then went to Eleanor's office to inform her of my decision; she was very abrupt. I said thank-you and left.

I proceeded to share the information that Ann gave me with my mother-in-law. Praise the Lord. For the next five days, Melinda continued to have physical, occupational, and respiratory therapy. We switched to thumbs-up for yes and thumbs-down for no. The next five days passed quickly. This brought us up to Melinda's last day at Presbyterian Hospital. This brought us up to a total of twenty-four days. We thanked Dr. Yonas and his staff, the Presbyterian staff, for an outstanding stay. Now we needed to get ready for the hard road to recovery. We had faith that Melinda would continue to progress.

Wednesday, May 21, Day 1 in HealthSouth Harmarville Rehabilitation Hospital, my mother-in-law and I eagerly awaited Melinda's arrival from Presbyterian Hospital by ambulance. The Harmarville facility was absolutely beautiful. Before long, Melinda arrived. My mother-in-law and I were conversing on the elevator about Melinda not being able to communicate verbally because of the trachea. My mother-in-law suggested that we give Melinda a pen and paper, so she got a pen and paper out of her purse and handed them to Melinda. She wrote very scribbly her name. My mother-in-law began to praise the Lord. We got off the elevator and went to unit 5, which was the transitional unit, and headed to room 5004 B to get Melinda settled in. She was exhausted from the ambulance ride.

My mother-in-law and I started putting pictures and cards on Melinda's bulletin board. As we were fixing Melinda's board, a transporter brought Melinda's roommate back from therapy. Her name was Kathy Lowe. Not long after that, two male nurses came into the room and introduced themselves as Jim and Tracey. They said that they would be Melinda's nurses for the shift. They also said that Dr. Mosley would be Melinda's physician, but it so happened that he was away on his honeymoon. Dr. Kay would be filling in for him. Tracey had to crush some of Melinda's pills in order to administer them to her. Other medication was in liquid form and needed to be mixed with water. It would then be pulled out with a big syringe, which then was placed into Melinda's feeding tube that was in her stomach. Melinda was taking eighteen medications each day, which were spread out. After her medications, Melinda received 50 cc of water that the nurses referred to as a flush, which helped Melinda as well as cleaned out the feeding tube. After medications, referred to as meds, were given, they gave her a bolus feeding. It contains all of the body's nutrients. Tracey opened a can of liquid nutrients and dumped the contents into an oblong plastic bag with a feeder line coming from it. The bag had to be squeezed to start the flow of the fluid into Melinda's feeding tube. My mother-in-law and I wanted to become familiar with every procedure. When Melinda had finished with her meal, the respiratory therapist gave her a breathing treatment, placing a clear mask over her nose and mouth with a little bowl filled with a breathing agent. The mask was then attached to compressed air for her to breathe into her lungs. They had to clean the mucus from Melinda's trachea before removing the disposable canula. Just before bedtime,

Melinda was placed on compressed air for breathing. There was a buildup of condensation in the plastic hose. We had to disconnect the hose from the trachea for a second in order to remove the moisture from the hose. Melinda's blood pressure had to be closely monitored. Jim and Tracey informed us that the next few days would be very hectic with testing. As they were leaving the room, Tracey asked us if we were Christians. We replied, "Yes, we are." And he said, "So am I." They said that if we needed anything to please call them. It had been a long day, so we gave Melinda a kiss and told her we loved her. Then we headed for home. On the way home, we discussed Father's Day being a couple of days away. This year, it just didn't seem special to me.

Melinda's schedule for the following day was going to consist of occupational therapy, physical therapy, and speech therapy. Melinda was very weak and frail. Her head was still swollen where she had the brain surgery. Her left eye was partially open. She stared to the extreme right. The right eye was still closed. She could barely hold her head up, and she constantly drooled. We had faith that with hard work, Melinda would regain some normalcy. We could just take one day at a time. So we went home and got a good night's sleep. We arose eager to face the day. We had arrived too early because they were just getting Melinda up for the day. The transporter was waiting to take Melinda to her first therapy, which was occupational. Her therapist was

Cristen. She worked with Melinda's upper body. I was so pleased to be by Melinda's side to encourage her.

Her mother looked on with excitement from the side chairs. After occupational therapy, Melinda had physical therapy with Pam. In watching Pam with the other patients, I was very impressed. However, about a week later, I saw a side of Pam that was not very professional. It caught me totally by surprise. I was standing by Melinda's side enthusiastically encouraging her, then out of the blue, Pam told me to go sit down. I paused for a second, went over to the chairs, and stood looking across the gym. Pam shouted at me and said, "I said sit down!" I stood with my arms folded, ignoring her command. After physical therapy, Melinda had a break for about an hour. So I took Melinda back to her room to rest. A few minutes later, Steve, the physical therapy technician, came to the room very upset and apologetic for Pam's behavior toward me. Steve pleaded with me to report Pam to her supervisor. Steve said that Pam had no right to talk to me in that manner. I replied no and that I did not want any harm to come to Melinda and that I would put Pam in the Lord's hands. While I was pushing Melinda in her wheelchair through the building, we ran into Pam. I confronted her regarding her behavior in the therapy room. Before she commented, I told her that I admired and appreciated what she was trying to accomplish with Melinda in the transitional unit. She commented that she was terribly intimidated by me.

I assured Pam that I was only there to support Melinda. Melinda wrote on her pad "Well done." I told Melinda that it was important that she continue to communicate by way of writing because this was a form of mental therapy and that our plan was to work very hard at it every day.

JUNE, 1997

I arrived at the hospital, they informed me that Melinda had pulled her trachea out. I was very upset. They said it was common when patients were getting better. I looked at Melinda's notepad. She asked them to take off the restraints from her hand. I checked with the nurse to confirm that they had used restraints on Melinda's right hand. She confirmed that they did. By this time, Melinda had received three reductions to her trachea size. She went from a size 8 to a 6 to a 4, and presently, she had a red cap. Which means when the red cap is on for so many hours a day, she is able to speak. Laura Hoerster, Melinda's speech therapist, had spent hours working with Melinda making sounds and such.

We met some super people who were working very hard to recover from their disabilities. We met Mr. and Mrs. Lowery and their son Jody, who had a severe head injury from an all-terrain vehicle. His family had faith that he would progress. We had the pleasure of meeting another fine couple named Mr. and Mrs. Cable. Their son Randy Jr. was savagely beaten with a brick, which caused severe brain injuries. We are praying along with his family for his recovery. Another fine couple that we met was Mr. and Mrs. Seelye. Their son Nate was in a terrible automobile accident. He was on his way to school with his family when some older students who skipped school ran a stop sign and hit Nate's car, nearly taking his life. Nate has a long road to recovery, but with faith and God's help, he will recover. We met more super nurses like Leslie, Jaime, and Scott who were born-again Christians. And we can't leave out Melinda's transitional unit case manager, Georgenne Hazlett. She would quite often ask Melinda how her goals were going, and Melinda would write on her notepad, "Everything is going fine."

On June 24, Melinda pulled out her trachea once again. Then on the June 26, they decided to take her trachea out. This was another big step toward Melinda's recovery. Once Melinda's trachea was taken out, she was able to talk; however, it was in a very low and whining fashion. I was very disturbed because I felt that there was something hurting her. I kept asking her if something was wrong. She would say in a high-pitch and whining voice, "No, nothing is wrong." It was becoming emotionally upsetting to me because I could not help her. Soon her therapist also became greatly concerned with her whining. They would constantly ask Melinda if something was hurting her. So the therapist made mention in her daily reports of Melinda's whining. Upon reading the reports, Dr. Mosley placed Melinda on Paxil, which is used for mild depression, anxiety, and mood swings. I kept very close track of Melinda's medication regimen. She was on eighteen medications. I kept telling myself that Melinda's brain was healing itself from the brain surgery. All of this came prior to Emile Jr.'s wedding day on June 28. Before Melinda became ill, she was very much involved with the wedding plans. After Melinda's illness, we were unable to proceed with her plans. I decided to give Emile and his wife-to-be half of what we had in the bank as their wedding present. My mother-in-law and I decided that she would stay with Melinda, and I would go and give Emile Jr. away in marriage.

The wedding day arrived. Ian, Justin, and I left home very early. During our drive to the town of Huntington where Emile Jr. graduated from Juniata College, the boys and I spoke about how sad we were that Mom could not be with us to experience her firstborn son's wedding. Ian, Justin, and I were to be in the wedding. However, I had mixed emotions because while my son was getting married, my wife was struggling just to survive. The wedding ceremony was beautiful, and the reception was one that we would always remember. We also taped the ceremony for Melinda. Our family members were well represented. Jennifer's family was also well represented. The bride and groom soon departed for their honeymoon. After saying good-bye to the honeymooners, we started on our way for home.

Upon our arrival, I called my mother-in-law to inform her of how beautiful everything went. The only problem was that my wife was not there. I asked my mother-in-law how the day went for Melinda, and she said she was a little whiney. I got a good night's sleep, and I awoke refreshed. I drove to Pittsburgh to be by my wife's side and to aid her recovery. Melinda had now been ill for a total of sixty-four days and in a Harmarville Rehabilitation Hospital transitional unit for forty days. This being Sunday, she did not have any therapy. During this lull in therapy, I asked the Lord to show me how I could assist Melinda in her recovery. I observed the way that the nurses fed Melinda through her feeding tube and how they flushed it. I also observed the way they took care of Melinda's personal needs, like changing her briefs. Because I did not want any skin breakdown, I personally washed Melinda from head to toe daily. I observed how Melinda was transferred from the bed to the wheelchair. I learned by watching. It gave us greater independence as we wheeled through the unit. I encouraged Melinda to raise her head by gently putting my hand under her chin, lifting it. This motion was repeated hundreds of times to control her drooling. Because Melinda's eyes were positioned facing the extreme right, we would wheel down the opposite side of the hallway.

I then would ask Melinda to describe the picture on the left side of the hallway. Doing this was a form of therapy to bring the eyes back to midline. We spent hours doing this. Additionally, I would place myself on Melinda's left side in order to have a conversation with her. I would also have Melinda holding conversations about what she would like the Lord to restore in her. I felt it was important for Melinda to express herself in writing, oftentimes asking Melinda to spell words for me. I believed that all of this would help her mind and body work together as one. Our plans were to work on this daily. When Melinda was placed in her wheelchair, she would not whine as much.

The next day I was going to talk to Melinda's case manager, Georgenne Hazlett, about setting up a meeting with Dr. Michael Sitting, the rehabilitation psychologist, concerning Melinda's whining. The next day I met with Georgenne, and she set up a meeting with Dr. Sitting. After the meeting, I went to Melinda's first therapy, which was physical therapy, to find that Pam, Melinda's physical therapist, was on vacation for the week. Pam's replacement was Teresa Barnett, who happens to be the head of the department. Teresa was very gentle with Melinda. She placed a splint on the back of Melinda's weak leg while two others helped Melinda to her feet. I watched as she took her first step. I kissed Melinda on her forehead and told her how proud I was of her.

June 30, was Melinda's sixty-fifth day of illness and her forty-first day at Harmarville. Melinda was so very frail and weak. Her bowels were very loose. They were so loose that I had to take her back to her room and change her three times myself. Melinda wrote on her notepad for the doctor to cut back on the Zorbitol, which was a laxative.

July, 1997

The next day, we met with Dr. Sitting. He evaluated Melinda; afterward, he said that he was very pleased and did not need to see Melinda on a regular basis but that he would recommend neurobehavior follow-up. As for the whining, he felt that the brain was healing itself. Our prayers were for Melinda to get strong enough to go downstairs to the more intense therapy. So she had to gain strength mentally and physically. That afternoon, Dr. Turner, the itinerant dentist, checked and cleaned Melinda's teeth. He was very complimentary of my love and care for my wife. He asked how long we had been married. I replied, "In six days, on July 8, we will have been married for twenty-five years." Also, on July 8, Melinda had a swallow test. We were hoping that she passed because if she did, it would be one step closer to getting the feeding tube out of her stomach, a step closer to eating real food by mouth.

On July 8, upon my arrival at the hospital, a nurse informed me that there was something at the nurses' desk for me. So I went to the nurses' desk to find a cake that read "Happy 25th Anniversary." It was from Dr. Turner and staff. I took the cake into Melinda's room to show it to her. She wanted a piece, but I could not give her any. I felt so bad. Please keep in mind that Melinda had not eaten anything by mouth for seventy-three days. I took the cake and asked that it be placed in the nurse's lounge and wrote a note of thanks. It was time for Melinda's swallow test. We were praying that she would pass. The test would show whether the fluids were going in the stomach and not in her lungs. When Melinda came out, I asked the technician if she passed, and she replied, "I am not at liberty to give that information. You must see the doctor." I found out that she passed. That meant that they could start Melinda on Jell-O and pudding. Melinda's speech therapist, Laura Hoerster, did a super job with Melinda. Two days later, Melinda had an appointment with Dr. Yonas, her neurosurgeon, in the city of Pittsburgh. Dr. Yonas was pleased with Melinda's progress. For three weeks, Melinda had good days and bad days, but the good days outweighed the bad. Her blood pressure was a concern, so they had to change some of the blood pressure medication.

On July 30, Melinda and I met with Georgenne Hazlett, Melinda's case manager, regarding her progress. The management team felt that Melinda had progressed enough to where she could withstand three hours of intense therapy. That was exciting news. Melinda was going downstairs to the head injury unit. By August 4, she had seen five roommates come and go: Katey Lowe, Shealy Bruce, Hereat Classic, Mary Soloman, and Sirrine Arlene. Now it was Melinda's turn to go. Melinda had been ill a total of one hundred days, seventy-five of them at Harmarville.

Melinda was placed in room 411-A on her first day in the head injury unit. They ran a battery of tests. The second day, Melinda and I went with Marianne Stritmatter, who would be Melinda's new case manager. Marianne wanted to talk about setting goals for Melinda to achieve. Melinda's therapy sessions started at eight to nine with occupational therapy. Her therapist was Bridget Thera. She worked with Melinda on daily living activities. Each unit had transporters; this person was responsible for taking the patients to their therapy session. Nine to nine thirty Melinda had nursing and breakfast in her room. Remember that Melinda could not eat anything by mouth. She had to be fed in liquid form through her feeding tube in her stomach. Nine thirty to ten thirty I would have them lay Melinda down for a rest before her next therapy session. Fifteen minutes before her next session, I would ring for someone to come and change Melinda so that she would be ready for the transporter to take her to her next therapy session, which was psychology of neurobehavior with Tina Bunyaratapan. From ten thirty to eleven and from eleven to eleven thirty was speech, language, and audiology with Laura Hoerster. Eleven thirty to twelve fifteen was nursing and lunch. Once again I requested that Melinda be laid down after her feeding and changed and gotten up at two thirty. This way she would be ready for her next therapy, which was physical therapy with Susan Bradley from three fifteen to three forty-five. Then after physical therapy, the transporter would take Melinda back to her room to be changed. The next one hour and fifteen minutes we would wheel up and down the long corridors, having Melinda describe pictures, continuing to encourage Melinda to keep her head up so she would not drool.

Melinda was so weak and frail, but she was determined to get better. This illness had literally stolen Melinda's beautiful smile away from her. I decided that every day I would say or do something to aid those facial muscles to return to normal. I slowly came to realize that Melinda, with the help of the Lord, was going to have to be trained to do everything all over again. Several weeks had passed. I could see some improvement in Melinda. She was getting stronger, her drooling had been reduced, and her vision had improved. I thank the Lord for being a school teacher. I have three months off in the summer. My in-laws would bring back clean clothes on the weekends. I am so very blessed to have in-laws who have been so supportive.

August, 1997

This coming weekend, the 24th, I had to move Justin's things to Waynesburg University. He was transferring from Penn State McKeesport Campus. When I began to move Justin into his dorm, I was very sad, and my heart was heavy. All that I could think of was that my lovely wife was not here to supervise and help Justin arrange the room. She had done it for Emile Jr. at Juniata College four years prior. After setting everything in the room, I gave Justin a big hug and told him that he had to do well for his mother in order to make her proud of him.

That evening when I arrived home, I called Harmarville Rehab Hospital to check in with my mother-in-law to see how Melinda's day went. She informed me that Melinda's day went well but her blood pressure was high. She also informed me that she would be at the Comfort Inn Motel in Harmarville. The next day after taking Justin back to school, my school started with a new teacher orientation, which I was not required to attend. So I set up a meeting with Marianne Stritmatter, Melinda's case manager, on Monday, August 25, 1997. That afternoon, Melinda and I met with Marianne. She said that the team felt that Melinda was nearing her peak as far as therapy. She said that she would lobby for more time. They also ordered a brace for Melinda's leg, but we had to buy the shoes in order to fit the brace. She also informed us that the insurance would only approve fourteen days at a time. I asked Marianne if the eighteen medications that Melinda was on were slowing her progress. She said she could not answer that question. I would have to ask the doctor.

At this point, Melinda had been ill for 121 days and spent 96 days at Harmarville. Not only was this a new school year for me, it was also Emile Jr.'s first year of teaching ninth grade academic English, and his lovely wife, Jennifer, teaches elementary school in Killeen, Texas. We are so proud of them both. Ian is in eleventh grade. He is starting the school year off well. He is going to work hard on his academics and participate in football. In having started the school year, I had to make a decision as to whether to coach seventh and eighth grade girls' basketball, which had to start the second week of school. I decided that from a financial viewpoint, I had no choice. I am ashamed to say this because in all the years that I have coached, I did it for the love of the game, not for money. It felt like I was in a pressure cooker. In having to manage Melinda's affairs, raise the children, teach, coach, pay the bills, and take care of the house, it left me no choice but to call on the Lord for help. I had a conversation with one of my Christian coworkers, Mrs. Gail Carlins, at lunch. I started telling her that I was mad at God for letting this happen to my wife. She shared a story that someone shared with her. She said because we are Christians, we are not exempt from illness or tragedy. During that conversation, a lightbulb came on in my head. How right she was.

September, 1997

Over the course of the week, I communicated with my mother-in-law by phone; she informed me that they had changed Melinda's schedule to include swimming (pool therapy), changed her medication for her blood pressure, and increased her Paxil to control her whining. Melinda had good days and bad days. My mother-in-law informed me that Melinda had gotten a roommate. Her name was Miss Idella Irwin. She also had an aneurysm. My mother-in-law also said that Susan, Melinda's physical therapist, was going to show me how to put Melinda's new brace on her leg and teach me how to walk Melinda. I knew that my mother-in-law was growing weary after attending to all of Melinda's sessions and being with her from the time she gets up until the time she goes to bed. So when the weekend comes, I relieve her.

When I arrived on Saturday morning, I went to Melinda's first session to find her not there. They said that they had to take Melinda back in the room and change her because her bowels were loose. They must have increased her Zorbitol. Melinda had difficulty moving her bowels on her own. It was mentioned Melinda may have needed a colostomy bag. I totally disagreed. I told Melinda when she felt that she had to do number 2, make a fist. When Melinda got back to therapy, she had lost about a half hour of therapy time. Susan went on to show me how to put Melinda's brace on and walk her. I was amazed at how small Susan was compared to my wife. She maneuvered Melinda so easily. At first, I found it very difficult to the point of perspiring. But I was determined to do all that I could do to assist with Melinda's recovery.

Melinda had always taken pride in her appearance. Her nails were always manicured and polished. My doing them for her, I felt, would aid her in her recovery. I would cut and trim Melinda's hair every other week. I wanted Melinda to feel good about her appearance. We as a family were so very blessed to have a family member with Melinda every waking moment of the day. We felt that this was necessary to keep Melinda from becoming depressed.

On September 16, Melinda's case manager, Marianne Stritmatter, called me at home after school to inform me that I should start looking for a skilled nursing home for Melinda. This had been Melinda's 141st day of illness with 116 of them spent at Harmarville. Three more weeks had passed. Melinda had advanced in her eating. She was up to fifteen spoonfuls of pudding a day. Laura was doing a great job of feeding Melinda as my mother-in-law looked on with loving encouragement. Laura also had Melinda trying to chew gum and suck a lollipop to stimulate Melinda's oral cavity. The bulk of Melinda's nutrients was still by way of her feeding tube.

I had checked with the four nursing homes that I had visited earlier during Melinda's illness to see what the bed availability was. There were very few beds available. My preference was the Fayette Health Care Center. I chose them due to my extensive research into that facility. I had called the Fayette Health Care Center from school to request a meeting with Jamey Kuritz, who is the director of admissions. I was able to reach her, and she said she would meet with me after school on Wednesday, October 15, 1997.

October-November, 1997

When I arrived, she was not in her office. I looked in the adjacent office to see if there was someone that I knew. His name was Mr. Jim Filippone, who was the executive director of the facility. He asked me what I was doing there and invited me into his office and offered me a seat. So I sat down and explained my situation to him. I also told him that I had scheduled a meeting with Jamey Kurita regarding possible placement for my wife. He assured me that when Melinda was discharged from Harmarville, there would be a bed for her. He paged Jamey to come to his office. He made her aware of the situation. She responded by telling me to let her know when Melinda was to be discharged. I said okay, and she left.

The next day, I received a call at the school. It was Marianne Stritmatter, Melinda's case manager. She was calling to inform me of Melinda's discharge date on Monday, October 27, 1997. She also asked me if I knew where Melinda was going. I told her that Melinda would be coming to Fayette Health Care Center here in Uniontown. I gave her Melinda's case manager's name, who would be Deb Kania, and her phone number. I also expressed my concern over Melinda's blood pressure being so erratic. I made arrangements to take a personal day off from school so that I would be available to be with Melinda when she got to Fayette Health Care Center. On Sunday, October 26, 1997, we packed up everything for Melinda's move to bring her closer to home. It was 180 days of Melinda's illness with 159 of those days at Harmarville.

October 27, was Melinda's first day at Fayette Health Care Center. Melinda's attending physician at the center was Dr. Pineda. I looked forward to working with him regarding Melinda's health. Melinda arrived at 10:30 a.m. She was immediately taken to room 249. We were all there waiting to be with her. Melinda was asked if she was ready to eat lunch, and she replied yes. I told the dietitian that Melinda had to have pureed food. I did not mention that Melinda had a feeding tube and that she had not eaten actual food for six months. At Harmarville, her speech therapist had worked her up to fifteen spoonfuls of pudding. I would take her down to the cafeteria and give her mashed potatoes and other soft foods. The 99 percent of Melinda's nutrients were coming by way of the feeding tube that was placed in her stomach. Deb Kania, the case manager, came in and informed us that each department would be running tests on Melinda tomorrow. Just as Deb left, they brought Melinda's tray. It consisted of mashed potatoes, green beans, and chopped steak; all was pureed. We watched her very closely to make sure that she didn't aspirate. We were hoping that Melinda would not have a reaction to the food after not eating for six months.

The next day, Melinda met with her speech therapist, Nancy Jo Gordon. My mother-in-law informed Nancy that Melinda had eaten her first meal in six months. She said that was great but there were a series of steps to bring Melinda along more slowly. Melinda was very weak and fragile. I was very concerned about Melinda's blood pressure being consistently high. Just being on eighteen medications was a concern. Out of all the skilled nursing facilities in the area, I felt confident that we had Melinda in the best place.

After the third day, my mother-in-law informed me that the physical therapist, Brenda Proud, put Melinda's brace on, and it took three people to walk her. After school, I would relieve my mother-in-law, look at Melinda's chart to see what her blood pressure was, and see if she had a bowel movement. Then I would proceed to put on her brace and lock the sleeves in the middle of the brace so that the brace would not bend at the knee. Melinda was not strong enough to hold her weight. We would walk out the room and down to the nurses' desk, which was about fifty feet, turn around, and come back to her room. After about a week, Brenda, the physical therapist, called a meeting to inform my mother-in-law, Ian, and myself not to be too optimistic about Melinda walking because her left leg was not following through. I told her that I appreciated her findings. However, I intended to continue walking Melinda until the leg did follow through. That weekend, I cut Melinda's hair and cleaned and polished her fingernails because I felt that it was good therapy. For Melinda, this was something that she took pride in. I decided I was going to maintain this activity every two weeks.

I was informed by a friend, Madonna Minor, that Patty Williams, who was not only my best friend Walter's sister but my adopted sister, had a severe stroke. This news devastated me. All I could do was pray for her recovery and keep abreast of Patty's progress. Melinda, being on the A wing, meant that she was receiving twenty-four-hour attention that was given to seriously ill patients. In my checking with the nurses, I was told that Rita Britt, the head nurse, was very knowledgeable about medications. So I went to Rita and asked about Melinda taking eighteen medications. She said she would look into this matter for me. Melinda could not take her medication by mouth. They had to be crushed and fed into her feeding tube. One of Melinda's goals was to take her medications orally. By this time, it was the end of November, and Melinda had been at the health center for twenty-nine days and 290 days in recovery. Our Justin would be twenty years old on November 24, just a few days before Thanksgiving. I checked with the nursing facility, Rita Britt, and her staff (Barbara Pokopec, Janet Cunningham, and others) to see if we could take Melinda out for a day, and our request was approved. The family was so excited about Melinda being able to go to my brother-in-law Marvin's home for our family dinner get-together. We felt that we had a lot to be thankful for.

When Thanksgiving Day arrived, we signed Melinda out for the day. We stopped by our house and then went to my brother-in-law's home for Thanksgiving dinner. All of Melinda's food had to be pureed. We had a great time and had so much to be thankful for.

I was very pleased with Melinda's progress in speech and occupational therapy. Her blood pressure was still a bit erratic. There were so many prayers offered up for Melinda from all across this land. There were missionaries form Hopwood Free Methodist Church, Mrs. Susan Lowe and Mrs. Mary Colley. Another church was Interfaith Assembly of God and their missionaries Gloria Johnson, Betty Jones, Linda Dantzler, and Terry Calloway. These missionaries would minister to Melinda in prayer and song.

December, 1997

ere we were, midway through the month. I received a letter from Highmark Blue Cross Blue Shield stating that Melinda would no longer be eligible for skilled coverage as of December 17, 1997. I was disappointed with this decision because my wife was in no condition to go home. The letter also stated that I had the right to appeal this decision. I got together with Deb Neal (head of the therapy department) and Deb Kama (Melinda's case manager) to put together an appeal letter. The letter consisted of reasons why Melinda should be kept in skilled care, such as her being on eighteen medications, her blood pressure continuing to run on the average of 172/103, a feeding tube, three meals taken orally, and being closely supervised to keep her from aspirating.

Just as we had done for Thanksgiving, I arranged for us to take Melinda home for Christmas, which typically was held at our home. Since Melinda's illness, we had dinner at my brother-in-law Ben Jr.'s home. Well, 1997 was over; 1998 was here. What a turbulent time it was, but the Lord brought us through it all. To date, Melinda has been at Fayette Health Care for sixty-seven days. Through the start of her illness, it had been 247 days.

January, 1998

On Sunday, January 4th, Reverend Howard Danzler was in the facility serving Communion. He stopped by Melinda's room and asked her if she would like him to serve her Communion. Melinda replied yes. Due to Melinda's condition, she had not been able to partake of Communion for nine months.

On January 9, I received a letter regarding my appeal; it was rejected. They stated in the letter that I had the right to appeal this decision in writing to the Grievance Review Committee within thirty days. The second appeal letter was formulated and sent. Meanwhile, the cost for Melinda to stay in skilled nursing care was $4,020 a month.

Several days later, Melinda was moved into private room 202 because of the number of visitors coming to see her. On Wednesday, January 14, Melinda took her medication by mouth. This meant that the pills did not have to be crushed and put into her feeding tube. January 20 was a special day that almost went by. I forgot my own birthday. Melinda came down with a bad case of the flu. Dr. Pineda started her on antibiotics. I was so concerned with Melinda being on all those medications. In working with Rita and Dr. Pineda, they were able to get Melinda off a few more medications. Melinda rebounded very nicely from the flu. Thank God!

FEBRUARY, 1998

Here we were, February 4th. It was our son Ian's birthday. He was seventeen years old. We celebrated his birthday with his mother in the nursing facility. We had ice cream and cake and had a lot of fun. The very next day, I received that second appeal letter rejection. I was truly troubled as to how I was going to come up with the financing for Melinda's stay. I immediately responded to the second rejection letter only to receive another letter, this time from the Grievance Review Committee. They had scheduled a hearing for February 12, at 11:15 a.m. The letter stated that I had the right to attend and present my views on the grievance. They also informed me that I had the right to have an attorney represent me at the hearing. Melinda had an appointment with her neurologist, Dr. Yonas, on February 12, at 10:30 a.m., which was a few blocks away from this meeting at Highmark Blue Cross Blue Shield corporate headquarters. The next day after working, I went directly to the nursing home to relieve my mother-in-law. Again, I told myself how blessed I was to have her by Melinda's side and mine. I kept her informed every step of the way. After Melinda ate and was settled in for the night, I went to the nurses' station and started taking notes. I recorded how many times her blood pressure medications were not given because her blood pressure was too low. Three of the medications alone were for blood pressure. The records clearly showed that Melinda's blood pressure needed special attention. I was convinced that if I had taken Melinda home back in December, it may have been deadly. After gathering data, it was about 1:30 a.m. I had to get home and get some sleep for school the next day. The next morning, I remember telling Lulu (the cafeteria supervisor), Linda (her assistant at Wharton Elementary School), and Lil (the cafeteria supervisor at AJ McMullen School) that I would fight for my wife as long as the good Lord kept renewing my strength.

Across the hallway from Melinda was one of my coworkers Lou Poli's mother, Mrs. Poli, who was a very charming elderly lady. The family had placed her there in order to build her strength. This particular day, she offered me an apple. She said it in broken English, "Here, you eat this apple. It's good for you." Sad to say, a few days after stopping in to see Mrs. Poli and her family, I was informed that she had passed away. My brief encounter with Mrs. Poli enriched my life. May she rest in peace. Melinda also was in with an old classmate from school, Vicki Gismondi's mother, Mrs. Gismondi, who also went on to her eternal rest. It was just a few days from February 12. I made arrangements to take a personal day off to accompany my lovely wife to her appointments.

In preparation for Melinda to be transported by ambulance to Pittsburgh, we were informed that only one person could accompany Melinda in the ambulance. I pleaded that my mother-in-law be permitted to go, and permission was granted. The date, Thursday, February 12, 1998, had arrived. I woke up nervous but confident. I drove over to pick up my mother-in-law and then drove over to the nursing facility. The nurse's aide Raimey Ruble had Melinda ready to go. Shortly after, the ambulance came. We all boarded it: Melinda, my mother-in- law, the two EMTs, and myself. I was armed with a camcorder and a personal cassette player and Melinda's documents.

Melinda's first appointment with Dr. Yonas, the neurologist, went very well. He was pleased with Melinda's progress. I had mentioned about all the medication that Melinda was on and asked if some could be removed. Thank God he took Melinda off two more. We arrived in downtown Pittsburgh on Fifth Avenue where the corporate headquarters of Highmark Blue Cross Blue Shield was. Security directed us to the parking area underneath the huge building. A gentleman with a black suit and an earpiece approached the ambulance. When we got out, the gentleman introduced himself as security for the building. As the EMTs were taking Melinda out of the ambulance, I was recording everything. They wanted to take Melinda up on the elevator to the Florida Room, which was on the third floor, but the gurney would not fit on the elevator. So security communicated someone from with upstairs, and they suggested to bring Melinda up on the freight elevator. A spokesperson for the insurance company approached me with her hand up in front of the camera, stating that I would not be permitted to tape the proceedings.

We had to wait about ten minutes for another hearing to end. I was dressed professionally, representing Melinda's husband, attorney, and doctor. Melinda was ushered into the boardroom by the two EMTs followed by my mother-in-law and myself, briefs in hand. In attendance at this hearing were a doctor, an insurance representative, a layperson, a stenographer, and a mediator. It was very evident that Melinda's presence was not expected. The mediator introduced everyone and gave me the opening remarks. I began by asking if anyone had any objection to my audio-taping the proceedings; two out of three had no problems with it. The doctor said that he was a little ambivalent and said to me, "Mr. Etheridge, you do realize that we have a court stenographer." I said to the doctor, "I appreciate that, but I would like this audio tape for my records." He replied, "Fine." I began covering my points of the meeting on behalf of Melinda, myself, and my family.

"We would like to thank you for the thousands of dollars you have spent trying to restore Melinda back to health. Melinda is here today not as YYZ04268-32 but as a real person." I went on to explain why Melinda should not be discontinued from skilled care. I presented facts and figures on Melinda's high blood pressure medications that were held for the month of January: Accupril was held seven times, Vasotec was held twelve times, Catapres was held six times.

"We, the family of Melinda, strongly believe that if we had taken Melinda home and had been giving her medications as prescribed, we would have killed her. This is why she needs to be kept in a professional facility until her blood pressure can be controlled. Melinda also needs to be monitored to make sure that she does not aspirate. I continued to pay Melinda's insurance through the Cobra Law, which is $295 a month, when her workplace insurance ran out. I have no choice but to continue Melinda's insurance because of the medication plan, which paid $2,029 a month for her medication. Now I am looking at $4,020 a month for Melinda to stay at the skilled facility. In conclusion to the Grievance Review Committee, on behalf of my lovely wife, Melinda, we are going to put your decision in God's hands."

The doctor made some closing remarks. The committee thanked me for sharing my concerns and assured me that they would be contacting me regarding their decision. We felt confident about the meeting. So we started our journey back home. This had been a long day for Melinda, and we all were very tired and hungry. Upon our departure from the ambulance, we thanked the two EMTs for their support. When we got back to Melinda's room, Mrs. Janet Cunningham, the head nurse, was on duty. She administered Melinda's medications while the two nurse's aides, Cynthia Fosbrink and Rita Cuppett, got Melinda settled in and fed. My mother-in-law stayed until Melinda went to sleep. I went to the Haky Funeral Home to pay my final respects to the Poli family. After an extremely long day, I finally got home to get some needed rest and to bring Ian up to date as to what was going on. I told Ian how proud I was of him being so mature in handling his mother's illness. I assured Ian that the Lord would bring us all through this difficult time.

The next day at school, my colleagues asked how everything went in Pittsburgh. I told them that we felt very confident and that we would know in five days. Meanwhile, Melinda's therapies were coming along nicely, especially speech. Melinda was closely supervised and eating well. She was made to eat slowly so that she would not aspirate. They were working with her eating by mouth in addition to her receiving nutrients by way of her feeding tube that was linked directly to her stomach. Our prayer was that Melinda could become strong enough to eat by mouth only. Five days had passed, and after school, I went to relieve my mother-in-law at the nursing home. After supervising

Melinda's dinner, putting her brace on her leg, and walking her up to the entrance to the lounge, we sat and talked, and I asked Melinda hundreds of questions. Then we started our journey back to her room, where I would get her changed and ready for bed; my day was complete knowing that my babe was at rest.

When I got home, I found Ian in bed. There was mail sitting on the table. The first letter I picked up was from the insurance company. I opened the letter hoping to find good news, but this was not the case. What I found was another rejection letter. I said to myself, *This is not acceptable.* I would have to investigate my next recourse. So the next day at school during my prep period, I called the insurance company. I was informed that I could appeal to the Commonwealth of Pennsylvania Department of Health. Within twenty-four hours, I had my appeal letter certified and off to the Commonwealth of Pennsylvania Department of Health. Meanwhile, there was a lot of work still to be done. Melinda was working hard to progress. She had picked up some weight and was getting stronger. We spent many hours walking, trying to strengthen the left side of her body. Melinda's brace had to be locked in the middle because Melinda's knee would not support her weight due to the brain surgery. From time to time, Melinda would ask for her bed to be raised or lowered. I inquired about this to Deb Kania, Melinda's case manager. She informed me that all the beds were manual in that facility. So this was something that needed to be checked into, along with the possible electric wheelchair for Melinda through the insurance company. Most of my taking care of Melinda's business had to be done from my workplace during my prep period. In checking with the insurance company, the request was denied. One thing about this insurance company was that they were consistent in their rejections.

⊷⟶◉⟵⊷

One evening, I went to see Ian participate in a basketball scrimmage, and I ran into a friend from the local newspaper, Mark. The first thing he asked me was "How is Melinda?" I replied, "She is still in the nursing home and coming along." He then asked me how I was doing. So I asked Mark if he had a few minutes. He said yes! I then went to my car and got the tape of the insurance grievance meeting for him to listen to. Halfway through the tape, I stopped and said, "I don't want to bore you." He insisted that I continue playing the tape. When Mark finished listening to the tape, he said, "This is ridiculous." He also said that he was going to bring it to the attention of the editor for a possible story. Mark told me to call him in a few weeks. Meanwhile, I informed Melinda's insurance, SelectBlue, that I had been in contact with our local newspaper and informed them of Melinda's grievance situation. A day later, I received a phone call at work from Melinda's insurance company stating that she would be receiving an electric bed and that someone would be coming to take the specifics for an electric wheelchair.

Thank you, Lord! When several weeks had passed, I called Mark and told him that things had changed in Melinda's favor. So as far as him pursuing a possible story, I felt that it was no longer necessary, and I thanked him.

I thank God for my faith in him, my family's faith, my colleagues' faith, and some of my wonderful students that I teach. Nichole Anderson was a student who would reaffirm my faith by telling me that she prays every day for my wife. She would give me homemade items to give to my wife. Gena Winning was another student who showed me her faith and support by telling me that she is praying for my wife each day that I had her for class. Jonathan Fearer would tell me every class period that I had with him that he was praying for my wife. Other students with well-wishes every time that I had them for class were Macy Shift, Michael Cessarino, Tom Bolen, and Katherine Lee. Two supportive sisters of faith were Janet Rishel, the secretary at Wharton School, and Joy Burd, the secretary at AJ McMullen School.

I was amazed by the number of people of faith who had surrounded us. One day, Mrs. Shift, the president of the PTO, came in to the teacher's lounge while I was eating my lunch. She wanted to ask me if it would be all right if the PTO had a fund-raiser for my family. I said absolutely not. She said, "This is our way of showing our love for you. We are aware of your wife's insurance situation." I was quite moved but still said no. The next day, there was a letter in my mailbox from Mrs. Shift telling me about their earthquake experience and the outpouring of love, and that afternoon, Mrs. Shift came to see me, and I agreed to the fund-raiser. She laid out the specifics; it was unbelievable.

March-April, 1998

Here we were, midway through the month. One morning after arriving at AJ McMullen Middle School, there was an announcement over the intercom; all teachers were to report to the teachers' lounge for a brief meeting. I remember sitting, waiting for all of the teachers to arrive. When they all got there, I was presented with a large sum of money that had been collected through a fund-raiser. This was all done without my knowledge. I was so moved I was speechless. The monies went to offset the cost of Melinda's escalating medical expenses.

I was so pleased with Melinda's progress to date. I felt that we were getting closer to getting the feeding tube out of Melinda's stomach. This would be the last medical device Melinda would have needed to aid her in her recovery Now, if only we could just get her blood pressure under control. I had been talking with Melinda about an upcoming event for our dear friend Patty Williams. It was going to be a benefit concert on Sunday, April 19,1998, at the YWCA facility. It was a very beautiful concert. It was quite a tribute to a fantastic human being. I would like to share this message that was on the program cover. "I know that the skies look gray; the way may look unsure, but Jesus has each step ordained. Your future is secure. Sometimes the greatest trials in life become the sweetest blessings; if we can only keep our faith, as we endure the testing. For in his way and in his time, he works things for our good; why can we always stand on this? …just because He said he would."

The very next day was Monday, April 20. I had taken a half day off from school to meet with Lisa Magnotti, Melinda's case manager from the insurance company, at the nursing home. The meeting went well! I spoke very candidly with Lisa about getting Melinda back into intense therapy at their sister facility, HealthSouth Mountain View in West Virginia. Lisa informed me that Mountain View was out of the network. She gave me the name and number of a rehabilitation liaison at HealthSouth Harmarville. Her name was Judy Burdine. On Tuesday, April 21, I called Judy, and I pleaded with her to come and evaluate Melinda for a possible return to Harmarville for intense therapy. She said that she would speak with the doctors and review the records. Judy agreed to meet with me on Thursday, April 23, at 1:00 p.m. So I arranged to take another half day off from school. At the meeting with Judy, she told me that she had spoken to the physical therapist at the nursing home. The therapist felt that Melinda had gone as far as she could go. Judy also, in talking with the doctors at Harmarville, felt that Melinda had peaked. I disagreed with their assessment. I thanked Judy for her time.

After the meeting with Judy, I ran into Melinda's case manager, Deb Kania. She asked me how the meeting went with Judy. I replied, "Not good. However, I am still going to try and get Melinda into HealthSouth Mountain View." Deb said that she had a friend who was the rehabilitation liaison there. I asked what this person's name was, and she said it was Vickie Triplett. I took it from there and called Vickie. In speaking with Vickie, I laid out Melinda's case. She said that she would have HealthSouth Harmarville fax Melinda's evaluation. In a day or so, Vickie got back with me and said that she had to go along with the findings. I said, "Please don't do that. I need you to evaluate Melinda yourself." She reminded me that Mountain View was out of her network, which meant that the insurance company would not pay. I then told Vickie that something would be worked out. She then agreed to come on April 27 to evaluate Melinda.

I had planned to use another half day of personal time. That would leave me with a half day of personal time for the rest of the school year. On Sunday, April 26, I checked Melinda out of the nursing home to visit our friend Jeff Tarpley in Greensburg. On this day one year ago, I was visiting Jeff in Pittsburgh when Melinda took ill in church. When Jeff saw Melinda enter in her wheelchair, he was visibly moved and said, "Praise God." We had a great day eating pizza that we ordered and singing hymns. As we left, we told Jeff that we would return soon and especially on our anniversary date like every year.

The next morning as I readied myself for school, I was praying that Melinda would receive a good evaluation from Vickie. Upon my arrival at the nursing home, I found Vickie had already arrived. She was in the room talking to my mother-in-law and Melinda. Melinda was in bed, so I got her up, and we walked out of the room and down the hall. As we walked, I explained to Vickie that Melinda had been dragging her left leg forward with my help. Now Melinda had recently started bearing weight without the sleeves of her brace being locked in place to support her. I was so excited for Melinda that I asked Vickie what she thought. She said that she saw some potential. I said, "Praise the Lord." Vickie said that she was very impressed with Melinda's attitude and willingness to work hard. So we walked back to the room. I laid Melinda down and sat down myself to talk with Vickie. I asked her if she was willing to call Melinda's case manager at Highmark Blue Cross Blue Shield and share Melinda's potential. Then I told Vickie that I would follow up with a phone call in a few days. We thanked Vickie for all of her help, and she said, "Good luck."

A few days had passed. I received a phone call at school from Vickie telling me that Lisa Magnotti, Melinda's case manager at Highmark Blue Cross Blue Shield, said she did not have the authority to okay Melinda to go to Mountain View in West Virginia. She also said that she would have to turn this matter over to her supervisor. After a few days had passed, I called Lisa, and she said that the request for Melinda to go to Mountain View was rejected. I asked Lisa for her supervisor's name and number. I called Ms. Burkhart; she asked me how I had gotten her number. She was annoyed. In turn, I asked her if she was aware of the name of Melinda Etheridge, and she said yes. I also asked her if she was aware that the local newspaper has an interest in this case. She said no. I felt that the return on our monies paid to the insurance company was weak. We were in dire straits.

MAY, 1998

On Thursday, May 7th, 1998, I received a phone call at school from Lisa Magnotti, informing me that Melinda had been approved for a ten-day trial period at HealthSouth Mountain View in West Virginia. I hung up the phone and praised the Lord. This was the very facility that I was trying to get Melinda placed into. When she was in Presbyterian Hospital, one of the first phone calls that were made was to Rhoda Dulany from Mountain View. It was some 351 days ago when she informed me that they did not have a subacute unit, so we were able to get Melinda into Harmarville where they had a transitional unit, which is the same as a subacute unit. During that same phone conversation with Lisa, she said that Melinda would have to report the very next day for admittance into Mountain View under the care of Dr. Russell Biundo. I was so excited that I could not wait to get to the nursing home to share the good news with my mother-in-law.

Upon my arrival, I went directly to Deb Kania, Melinda's case ,manager, and told her of the good news. Deb said that they could not guarantee that there would be a bed for Melinda when she was discharged from Mountain View. I told Deb that I was praying that we were going to take Melinda home upon her discharge from Mountain View. We still had some financial concerns. Before leaving Deb's office, she handed me some literature about the United Cerebral Palsy Attendant Care Program. I told Deb that I could never repay her for all the hours that she gave me trying to help Melinda. I finally made it to the room to tell Melinda and my mother-in-law the exciting news. So we began packing up Melinda's belongings. By the end of the night, we had everything ready to be transported to Mountain View. Also, we had the things that needed to be taken home with the exception of Melinda's electric bed, which we planned to move the upcoming weekend when Justin, our middle son, came home from college at Waynesburg University.

When I arrived home after midnight from the nursing home, I woke Ian up and shared the good news about his mother going to Mountain View for rehab. Then I checked the answering machine to find a message from our oldest son, Emile, saying that his wife Jennifer was in the hospital in labor. It was that day, May 8, 1998, that our granddaughter Arielle was born. That morning, I could not wait to tell Melinda and my mother-in-law about our new granddaughter. Melinda was so very excited. My mother-in-law was also excited, this being her first great-grandchild. On the afternoon of May 8, Melinda was admitted to HealthSouth Mountain View Rehabilitation Hospital. What a blessing to have Melinda so close to home, only twenty-nine miles away. My mother-in-law made arrangements to stay at the Days Inn so she could be close to Melinda. Because of my teaching schedule, I would go down to the hospital on the weekend. I finally had the opportunity to meet Dr. Biundo. What an enthusiastic person he is. I expressed my concern about all of the medications that Melinda was on, and he said that he would be looking toward adjusting and possibly discontinuing some. In addition, I inquired about the possible removal of Melinda's feeding tube. He stated that he would look into this matter. I inquired about pool therapy for Melinda. My final request was for Melinda to have the most demanding therapist working with her. A week had passed, and Melinda was enjoying herself. The amazing Dr. Biundo had weaned Melinda off nine medications from a total of thirteen previously. Melinda was much more alert now; she had more energy, and her blood pressure was excellent. My mother-in-law attended every one of Melinda's therapy sessions.

On Monday, May 18, when I got to Wharton School, I was met at the door by the president of the PTO, Mrs. Shift, who presented me with two checks, one from the

Wharton PTO, of a substantial amount of money to assist me with Melinda's medical expenses. This money was received through a fund-raiser. The other check was from Mr. H. W. Whyel and family, which was also a very generous donation. These contributions moved me deeply.

This same evening when I got home, there was a message on the answering machine. It was a call from Melinda's case manager, Rita D'Aurora, from Mountain View, who left a message that the insurance company had extended Melinda's stay another seven days. What great news! When I arrived on Saturday morning, I picked up Melinda's therapy schedule. Her first therapy session was speech; the therapist's name was Teresa Barnett. This young lady was excellent. She said that she was so impressed with Melinda's hard work and intelligence. Teresa had mentioned that Melinda had shared her having a background in speech therapy. Teresa went on to say how impressed she was with our strong family support for Melinda. Melinda's next session was occupational; her therapist was Scott Lavery. He too did an outstanding job with Melinda. He would say, "Hey, Melinda, let's get jiggy with it." Melinda would just laugh. Then they would go to work. Melinda's last session was for physical therapy with Lisa Ammons. Lisa was just the match that I had requested for Melinda. She was very demanding. During Melinda's session, Lisa informed me that Thomas Pacak from NovaCare, an advanced orthopedic technologies provider, would be coming in today to measure Melinda for an AFO brace. I was so pleased with Melinda's progress I just thanked the Lord for the strength to fight this battle for her. That evening, we took in some activities that were scheduled for the patients. We had a super evening.

The next day was Sunday. Melinda just had short sessions of occupational and physical therapies. I took Melinda back to her room. The nurse was waiting for Melinda to give her medication. Her name was Cindy Jordan. Cindy said that she lived not too very far from us and that her daughter and our middle son, Justin, were high school friends. I took care of Melinda's personal needs, and off we went to a church service held at the facility. We had a wonderful time praising the Lord. I had a great weekend with my babe. Every night, I spoke with my mother-in-law to see how Melinda's day went. She said that she was pleased and that Melinda had received her brace and the therapist was working with her. On the seventh day of Melinda's extension, Wednesday, May 27, 1998, I spoke to my mother-in-law, expecting her to tell me that they were going to discharge Melinda. Instead, she told me that the doctor had taken Melinda's feeding tube out. I was jumping for joy and praising the Lord. The next day, I received a phone call at school from Melinda's case manager, Rita D'Aurora, informing me of Melinda's third extension from the insurance company. I thanked the Lord. I went to the lunchroom and shared the good news with my colleagues. They were so happy for

Melinda and me. While eating lunch, I was talking to Don Bell Jr. about my roof leaking and other areas of discussion.

Upon my arrival home, I was sharing the good news to Ian about his mother. That evening, I received a phone call from Mr. Robert Formentelli, a math teacher from the high school in the school district where I teach. Mr. Formentelli said that he had a conversation with Don Bell Sr. and found out about my leaking roof. Mr. Formentelli told me that if I would purchase the materials, he knew some teachers who would want to help with the roof. Within three days, we had a beautiful new roof on our house thanks to Don Bell Sr., Don Bell Jr., James Bodnar, Peter Bozick, Jack Breakiron, Clarence Checton, Matt Freas, William Freas, Brian Hasson, Douglas Lowe, Patrick Lowe, Regis Rubis, John Shields, David Shuck, and Timothy Tracy.

The Lord was truly blessing us. Melinda was well into her third extension when I realized that I would have to check into the attendant care program through the cerebral palsy. I read all the literature that Deb Kama had given me from the nursing home. I learned that there were certain criteria to be met. I called Cathy Brown, the director of UCP, and I explained Melinda's situation to her. She went into specific details about the program. As she was talking, I thought of the perfect person to be my wife's attendant care person. That person was one of our church sisters who loves the Lord and who loves Melinda, Sister Freelon Davis.

Ms. Brown said that Melinda may be a candidate for the program under Mrs. Robin Dorogi. Since the school year was soon coming to an end, I was trying to think ahead and be ready for the next school year.

June, 1998

Everything was set to bring Melinda home. On Tuesday, June 2, 1998, I received a phone call from Melinda's case manager, Rita D'Aurora, reminding me that Melinda was scheduled to be released in two days; however, the insurance company had extended Melinda another eighteen days. She also said this was the final extension. Her discharge date would be June 22, 1998, at twelve o'clock. I find it ironic that when we were appealing to the insurance company decision to cut Melinda from skilled care at the nursing home, there were four appeals that were rejected. Now she had received four extensions to complete her stay at Mountain View Rehabilitation Hospital. Now that Melinda had eighteen days left, I was going to check into seeing about getting Melinda into pool therapy. The pool was located next to the therapy room. So I walked across the therapy room to the swimming pool. I spoke with Robert Dunlevy. He told me that he would talk to his supervisor and get back to me on Monday if she was eligible.

Now that school was out for the summer, I could focus 100 percent of my attention on Melinda. This would enable my mother-in-law to once again spend her weekdays at home. We had another great weekend. We attended all of the entertainment on Saturday and attended church services on Sunday. We ate terrific meals in the cafeteria and had visits from family members. We thanked God for being in control. Early Monday, I looked forward to walking Melinda over to the cafeteria and having breakfast with her. I had to cut Melinda's food in small pieces and encourage her to eat and drink slowly to prevent her from aspirating. She was taking all of her nutrients in by mouth and not through a feeding tube. Melinda was interviewed by the infection disease control department to see if she was all right to enter the pool. After reviewing her records, she was rejected due to a statement in her file from a nurse saying that she was incontinent, which meant that Melinda could not control her bladder. If she were to relieve herself in the pool, they would have to shut the pool down and drain it. But I disagreed with their assessment. I knew that Melinda could tell me when she had to urinate. So I went to the supervisor of infectious disease control department, who said that there was nothing she could do about it. She was following the nurse's statement. So I went to the head of nursing and informed her of Melinda's ability to use the restroom. She replied, "Not by the daily charts we keep." I had to accept that statement until I could prove it wrong. So the very next day when I arrived, I told Melinda every time that she had to go to the restroom, she had to let me know, whether she was in therapy or not. We started early that morning; every time Melinda told me that she had to go to the restroom, I would take her. Throughout the day, every time Melinda went, I would see to it that a nurse would record and initial it. So by the end of the night, we had a complete chart of Melinda being continent. I felt the need to remove the chart from the wall and make a copy of it for my own personal records. The next day, I went to the infectious control supervisor and requested that she look at Melinda's chart from the previous day. She said she would send for it, and I told her that I would get back to her after lunch. After lunch, the supervisor told me that Melinda was approved for pool therapy. I thanked her and hung up the phone and shared the good news with Melinda. She was very happy and was able to start pool therapy the next day. Thank the Lord for his staying power.

The next day when I arrived, I picked up Melinda's schedule, and she was scheduled for the pool as her last therapy for the day. After all the therapy throughout the day, she was ready to go into the pool. I got Melinda dressed and took her over to the pool. Her therapists were Robert Dunlevy and Brian Sherlock. Melinda really enjoyed the pool. I was praying that we would see some movement from the left side eventually. When I arrived home that evening, I called my mother-in-law to brief her about the day. I received a call from one of my coworkers, Debbie Rittenhouse. She told me that she had shared Melinda's health situation with her sister Karen King, who is a strong Christian lady. Debbie went on to tell me that Karen had terminal cancer. Debbie said that Karen was wondering if I would mind if she and her husband, Brian, could visit and pray for Melinda. I said, "Certainly, please have them come this weekend."

Time was passing quickly; before we knew it, the weekend was upon us. It was Sunday, June 7, 1998. Karen, her husband Brian, and two friends Allen and Marlene came to spend a few hours with us. Later that evening, my brother-in-law Deacon Marvin Wright and his lovely wife, June, stopped by. Marvin informed Melinda that he was organizing a benefit for her. It would be held at the YWBA in Uniontown on Saturday, June 13. We were sharing with June and Marvin how pleased we were with Melinda's progress. The evening drew to a close. We all held hands, and Marvin led us in prayer. Later that week, we noticed more movement on Melinda's left side. We were so happy.

As the date of Melinda's benefit grew closer, we were all getting excited. She was going to see people that she had not seen in over a year: coworkers, community people, church members, and well-wishers. I had to make arrangements for Melinda to be released for the benefit. On the evening of the benefit, Melinda and I drove about a half hour to get to the YWBA from Mountain View. When we arrived, people were filing in. We went up to the front seating area. The program began with our reverend Leonard Kirby, who was the master of ceremonies. There were well over two hundred people in attendance. Reverend Leonard Kirby opened with a prayer, then the City Chapel Choir sang, the New Beginnings Choir sang, then there was a solo by Marva Kirby. Mount Olivet sang a solo by Carl Jackson, followed by a song by Mount Zion Baptist of Leckron and a solo by Linda Dean. Saint Paul sang, and then there was a call to discipleship and family remarks. Melinda was moved because of the overwhelming turnout and support. She expressed her feelings and love for all that attended her benefit. I also expressed my love and appreciation for everyone taking time out of their busy lives to support their dear friend. Mr. Edward Lyons, the CEO of the Private Industry Council, which was the overseer of the Fayette County Head Start Program where Melinda was the assistant director, had some compelling comments about Melinda. He said that Melinda was a team player, a very competent, intelligent, hardworking individual who would get the job done and who was very well respected by all. Reverend Kirby gave the closing remarks and thanked everyone for sharing in the benefit. Afterward, people came up to Melinda and showered her with hugs and kisses. They also wished Melinda well. When the evening ended,

Melinda and I had a half-hour drive back to Mountain View. Melinda was exhausted. We thanked the Lord for the evening; it was a glorious time.

The next eight days went by fast. On Monday, June 22, 1998, Melinda was discharged from Mountain View Rehabilitation Hospital in Morgantown, West Virginia. What was initially to be a ten-day trial period had turned into a 46-day stay. Our family was elated to have Melinda home after 24 days at Presbyterian Hospital, 159 days at Harmarville Rehabilitation Hospital, 193 days at Fayette Health Care Facility Nursing Home, forty-six days at Mountain View Rehabilitation Hospital in West Virginia, and 422 days away from our loving home. God was right. He said he would never leave us or forsake us. He kept his promise. I was mad at God, but I have come to the realization that God is good all of the time. Melinda's testimony about her journey comes from a song that she led in church.

> God's grace and mercy brought me through
> I'm living this moment because of you
> I want to thank you and praise you too
> Your grace and mercy brought me through